Pebble® Plus

Hands-On Science Fun

How to Build a
TORNADO
in a BOTTLE

Revised Edition

by Lori Shores

Consultant: Ronald Browne, PhD
Department of Elementary & Early Childhood Education
Minnesota State University, Mankato

4D

Download the
Capstone 4D app
for additional content.

4D See page 2
for directions.

CAPSTONE PRESS
a capstone imprint

Download the Capstone 4D app!

- Ask an adult to search in the Apple App Store or Google Play for "Capstone 4D".
- Click Install (Android) or Get, then Install (Apple).
- Open the app.
- Scan any of the following spreads with this icon:

When you scan a spread, you'll find fun extra stuff to go with this book!
You can also find these things on the web at www.capstone4D.com
using the password: **tornado.09441**

Pebble Plus is published by Capstone Press,
1710 Roe Crest Drive, North Mankato, Minnesota 56003
www.mycapstone.com

Library of Congress Cataloging-in-Publication Data
Names: Shores, Lori, author.
Title: How to build a tornado in a bottle / by Lori Shores.
Description: [2018 edition]. | North Mankato, Minnesota:
    Capstone Press, [2018] | Series: Hands-on science fun |
    Series: A 4D book | Audience: Age 4–8.
Identifiers: LCCN 2017044222 (print) |
    LCCN 2017048004 (ebook) |
    ISBN 9781543509564 (eBook PDF) |
    ISBN 9781543509441 (hardcover) |
    ISBN 9781543509502 (paperback)
Subjects: LCSH: Tornadoes—Juvenile literature. |
    Science—Experiments—Juvenile literature.
Classification: LCC QC955.2 (ebook) |
    LCC QC955.2 .S54 2018 (print) | DDC 551.55/3078—dc23
LC record available at https://lccn.loc.gov/2017044222

Editorial Credits
Marissa Kirkman, editor; Sarah Bennett, designer;
Tracy Cummins, media researcher; Tori Abraham,
production specialist

Photo Credits
Capstone Studio: Karon Dubke, Cover, 3, 5, 6, 7, 9, 11, 13, 15,
19, 21; Dreamstime: Chris White, 17; Shutterstock: ArtMari,
Design Element Cover and Interior, Rafai Fabrykiewicz, 4-5
Background

Note to Parents and Teachers

The Hands-On Science Fun set supports national science
standards related to physical science. This book describes and
illustrates building a tornado in a bottle. The images support
early readers in understanding the text. The repetition of words
and phrases helps early readers learn new words. This book
also introduces early readers to subject-specific vocabulary
words, which are defined in the Glossary section. Early readers
may need assistance to read some words and to use the Table of
Contents, Glossary, Read More, Internet Sites, Critical Thinking
Questions, and Index sections of the book.

Printed and bound in the United States of America.
010772S18

Table of Contents

Getting Started 4

Making a Tornado in a Bottle 6

How Does It Work?. 16

Glossary 22

Read More. 23

Internet Sites 23

Critical Thinking Questions 24

Index 24

Safety Note:
Please ask an adult for help in building
your tornado in a bottle.

Getting Started

The rain pours

and the wind roars.

Tornadoes can be scary.

But there's nothing scary

about a tornado in a bottle.

2 clear 2-liter plastic bottles, clean

duct tape

3 cups (¾ liter) of water

blue food coloring

5

Making a Tornado in a Bottle

First, remove the labels from two 2-liter bottles. Then mix a few drops of food coloring into 3 cups (¾ liter) of water. Pour the colored water into one of the bottles.

Place the empty bottle

upside-down on top

of the first bottle.

Line up the openings.

Use duct tape to cover

the necks of the bottles.

Wrap the tape tightly

so the bottles

won't come apart.

Turn the bottles over
so the water is on top.
Watch as the water moves
slowly to the bottom.

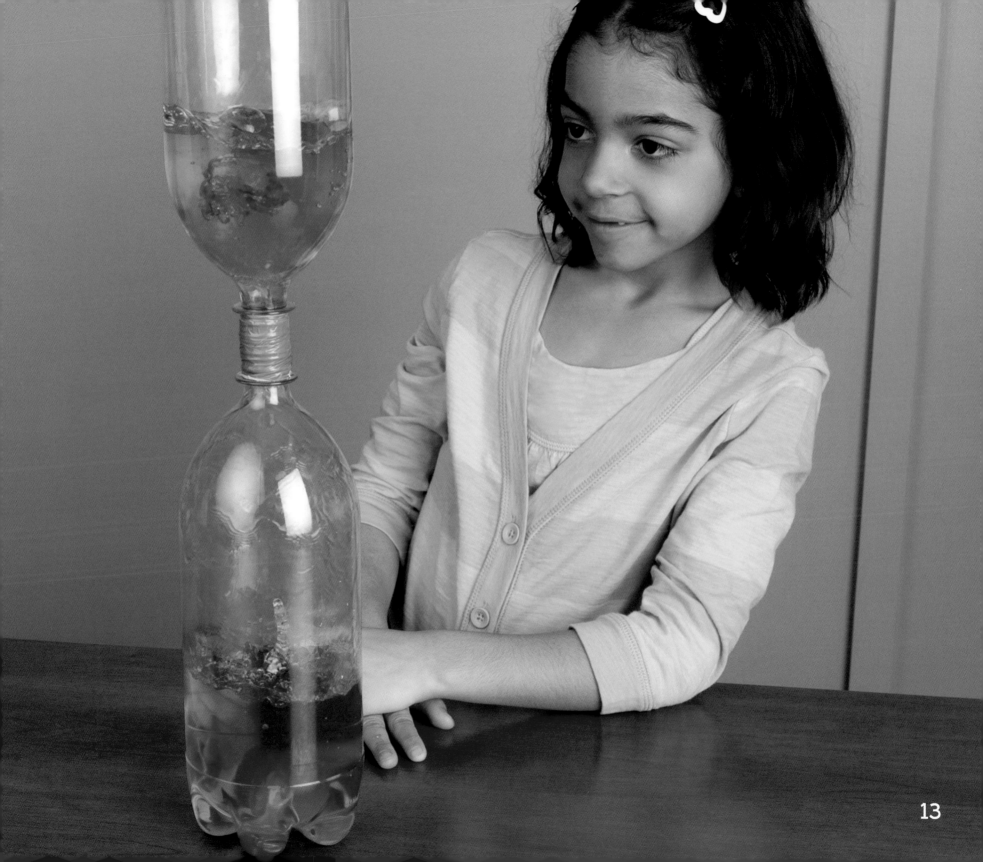

Turn the bottles over again.

Quickly swirl the bottles
in a circle a few times.
Watch as a tornado appears!

How Does It Work?

Real tornadoes happen

when hot air pushes up.

Wind whips around

a center point,

pulling cold air down.

wind

cold air

hot air

The tornado in the bottle works in a similar way. When the bottles are turned over, the air pushes up.

air

Swirling the bottles around
makes the water spin
around the center hole.
Like wind, the movement pulls
the water down.

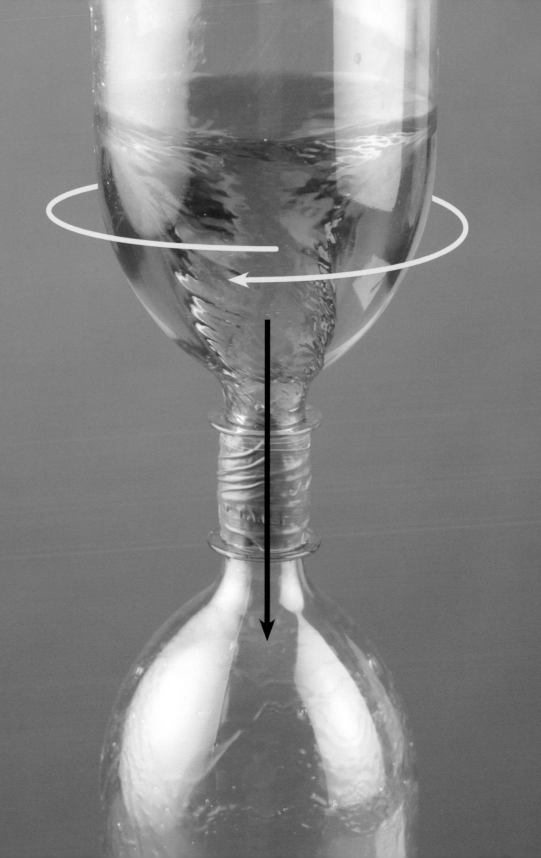

Glossary

roar—to make a loud, deep noise

similar—alike

swirl—to quickly move around in circles

whip—to quickly move with great force

Read More

Brunelle, Lynn. *Big Science for Little People: 52 Activities to Help You and Your Child Discover the Wonders of Science.* Boulder, Colo.: Roost Books, 2016.

Smibert, Angie. *Mind-Blowing Physical Science Activities.* Curious Scientists. North Mankato, Minn.: Capstone Press, 2018.

Sohn, Emily. *Experiments in Earth Science and Weather with Toys and Everyday Stuff.* Fun Science. North Mankato, Minn.: Capstone Press, 2016.

Internet Sites

Use FactHound to find Internet sites related to this book.

Visit *www.facthound.com*

Just type **9781543509441** and go.

Super-cool stuff! Check out projects, games and lots more at www.capstonekids.com

Critical Thinking Questions

1. Why is it important to wrap the tape tightly around the necks of the bottles?

2. What happens to the air inside when the bottles are turned over?

3. How does swirling the bottles around help to create a tornado inside of the top bottle?

Index

air, 16, 18

duct tape, 10

food coloring, 6

labels, 6

pouring, 6

rain, 4

swirling, 14, 20

taping, 10

tornadoes, 4, 14, 16

water, 6, 12, 20

wind, 4, 16, 20